Painter, Poet, Mountain

Painter, Poet, Mountain
After Cézanne

Susan McCaslin

QUATTRO BOOKS

The publication of *Painter, Poet, Mountain* has been generously supported by the Canada Council for the Arts and the Ontario Arts Council.

 Canada Council for the Arts Conseil des arts du Canada

 ONTARIO ARTS COUNCIL
CONSEIL DES ARTS DE L'ONTARIO
an Ontario government agency
un organisme du gouvernement de l'Ontario

Cover painting: "Mont Sainte-Victoire" by Paul Cézanne
Cover design and typography: Diane Mascherin
Editor: Allan Briesmaster

Library and Archives Canada Cataloguing in Publication

McCaslin, Susan, author
    Painter, poet, mountain / Susan McCaslin.

Poems.
Issued in print and electronic formats.
ISBN 978-1-988254-22-7 (paperback).--ISBN 978-1-988254-23-4 (PDF)

        I. Title.
PS8575.C43P35 2016   C811'.54   C2016-905029-7
                                          C2016-905030-0

Published by Quattro Books Inc.
Toronto
www.quattrobooks.ca

Printed in Canada

Works of art are always the result of one's having been in danger,
of having gone through an experience all the way to the end,
to where no one can go any further.

– Rainer Maria Rilke, from *Letters on Cézanne*

We are a dazzling chaos. I stand before my motif, I lose myself in it.

One minute in the life of the world is going by. Paint it as it is!

– Paul Cézanne

for J.S. Porter

Contents

The Good News from Aix

I am again that ten-year-old
            staring up with my father
                        at the starry sky

and he, a wondering engineer   who first named me the heavens –
            Orion   Pleiades
                        Milky Way

every particular counting   like today in Aix-en-Provence

            when the slide of sorbet down my throat
                        woke words

then   the beatitude of Skyping
            my brother in Washington State
                        husband in British Columbia

under sacred Mont Sainte-Victoire
            that beckoned Paul Cézanne
                        to amber quarries

where peering at sandstone blocks
            he invented Cubism
                        (before Picasso)

Closing my eyes
            sleep wakes
                        star canvas pirouettes

in the field
            of the inner eye
                        (where things commune)

where   in a tough   listening stance
                        (not quick to name)
                                    the names sometimes appear

Cézanne's Apples

Rounded sequences of sheen

                                                  blush-green and russet

just where he left them   conversing

                         corporeal

                                                counteracting planes

vanished vanishing points

                              hundreds of brushstrokes

tang orange

                  pang green

                                            wet colours self-adjusting

        to an entire tableau

holding tension of surface and field

                         in the wholeness

                                        paints sometimes hold

Seeing Seeing

Whether an apple
                              new or just turning to decay
                (waxy oblong rotund)
                              or the fallen-into-stone bodies of enormous bathers
he painted interbeing:

the wild and fluid mergings
                              of world with eye

(his wife Hortense
                the gardener Vallier)

not just his reflections on subjects
                              but his engagements
                                            with the temperaments of things leaving

staying with transience to the end
                              (which might be why so much in his work is
                              unfinished
                                            for what's an end?)

Seeing into essence   gave him patience
                                            or patience gave him power
                (His paintbrush was his meditation mat)

His productions
                seemed to the Salon de Paris
                              travesties of crudeness

He didn't mind showing his brushstrokes
                                            globbed on the paint
refused to sustain the illusion
                that he was absorbed in anything other than *impasto* –

                one trowel after another
                              at being

He is flint
  when it comes to the process

which is why I love him
  (perhaps just what one shouldn't say in a poem)

his determination
    not to care about closure, approval

his letting go   into
      sheer presence
        shearing away at time

  seeing into the process of seeing

      (If he had been born blind, he would have seen)

I Close My Eyes

to hear

          the effortful

               effortless

breathing of his   blunt brush

not what is seen

          but the silences

before   in   after   within

          seeing

On Coming Late to the Shock of Modernism
(*Large Pine and Red Earth*)

Modernism   already a convention   when I was twenty
         so to me   not so bizarre

(so disquieting)   as these Cézannes
         not so electric (eclectic) as
                           this stark wild pine
waving its mandala arms
                    from red earth
                           (root-warming purple puffs at its base)

Stalled   I hear the old command:
         "You must change your life"
                           (the one whispered to Rilke from a Rodin)
but know   (too late)
                    it has already changed

No way   to keep naming the colours
                           as poets try to do
                                 when caught in the whoosh

Something tips into itself and
over
                    losing both name and address

The pine   a dizzying galaxy   on the road

Paints keep excavating time   saying
                           "We're here
                                      nothing's finished
hop in"

Just because the artist stayed   *sur le motif*
         you feel
                    this now-second's
                           strangely familiar
                                      pounce

In the Steps of Cézanne

I go into the country every day. The motifs are beautiful and I spend my days better here than elsewhere.
— letter from Paul Cézanne to his son, Aix, Sept. 22, 1906

Everywhere in Aix there are
        small brass plaques
                in the shapes of footprints
        bearing the letter "C"
                    pressed into the pavements

If you go you'll see what I mean
        when I say he's omnipresent
                    (like God or the holy ghost)

You can't avoid him
                    (but that's not too bad a thing)

You'll start to want him around
        like an old friend you almost took for granted

If you head to the *Office de Tourism*
        there's a glossy brochure
        a website with links
        on how to walk in the steps of Cézanne

These poems won't tell you what you can't find out yourself
        so best go there in person
        and if not   just try to imagine

Google his Wikipedia page or "Cézanne in Aix"
        and you'll see a pic of his statue in the Rotunda
                giving a post-impression of what he was like
                treading the streets with his stick and paint kit

You may take a tour
        study his works at the Musée Granet
                linger inside his atelier with the Cupid *bibelot*
                the fruit bowl   the skulls

You might wander the Bibémus quarries
                where limestone first entered
      his bloodstream
      or ascend Mont Sainte-Victoire
                        his holy mountain

      search for his tomb at the Cimetière Saint-Pierre
      where someone has placed a moulding apple beside a fresh one

You might not know how many have preceded you
      (Picasso, Stein, Hemingway
      Lawrence, Heidegger
      Merleau-Ponty, Derrida
      Beckett, Heaney   more

      along with the nameless bohemians, hippies
      waifs and wanderers
      art students and scholars
                gypsies and tourists)

I, late-comer   say
      how he slipped into my eye
      won me with his weird doggedness
      stubborn isolation
          his sculpted *Grand Bathers*
          intense self-portraits
          quirky not-wanting-to-be-touched
          while allowing his colours
          to touch each other so intimately

Soon you won't be able to separate the story from the art
      or escape finding yourself
                on pilgrimage
                     trailing always

so many steps behind

For All My Artist Friends

When you're feeling blue
                              just remember
                                          even Paul Cézanne
                                                        had to do time
in the *Salon des Refusés*

The Politics of Art, or,
You May Call Me a Dreamer

Cézanne was a draft resister
evading conscription during the Prussian war

Sometimes I wonder:
if
everyone
    everywhere
through some improbable
      fortuitous *fiat*
of grace, determination
    and longing
could place the entire
    energy
       of their attention
into some creative
    intuitive
thinking-feeling
    enterprise

like Paul Cézanne did

      might war end?

Epistolary Poetics

You have chosen the brush and you have done right, because everyone
must follow his bent ... But allow me to mourn the writer who dies in you ...
Instead of the great poet who is walking out on me give me at least a great painter ...
  – Émile Zola to Paul Cézanne, Paris, Aug. 12, 1860

In his early letters to Zola, it's clear
                    Cézanne could write
lubricating his word-horde
                          with Latinisms, Horatian epigrams, translations
challenging Zola to produce *bouts-rimés*

Okay, says C, send me some alexandrines rhyming
Zola et Voilà   metaphore et phosphore

Hanging over the exchange
I want into their game

When C signs off as
        Paulus Cezanius
to his carissime Zola
            just sign me up for
            some Bohemian doggerel
            & orthographic phantasmagorias

Now it seems the art of letter-writing
has nearly died
though occasionally our emails shine

If not for Cézanne's
insistent eye
he might have embraced his poetry Muse

Today I celebrate
Cézanne the painter
and the painter who died
in me at twelve to birth another
                    poetry slave

The Progress of His Turbulence

There's no doubt about Cézanne's early intensity
                    bare and brazen in *The Orgy*
                                        where flesh flings itself
over a banqueting table
                            overhung with volatile
                                        Delacroix clouds
or in *The Abduction*
                            where a bronzed man
forever hoists white female flesh
                                        into the abyss

The self-portraits, portals
                        to dark contours

thick strokes
heavy lines
black mood-streams

as if Impressionism needed to ground itself in gravid geometries

Then
slowly   he allows
            the human figures to recede from the landscapes
            while the landscapes
                        foreground   and   quicken

transforming all that roiling energy
without dwarfing or diminishing it

just holding it in a determined
                                gentleness
a turbulent calm
            where his poised, androgynous bathers will at last
                                        return to the land

Exacting Exactitudes
(a found poem based on an anecdote by Ambroise Vollard)

When I stepped inside
Cézanne's studio in Paris
I confess to some misgivings
on noting the chair
where I was expected to climb
to pose for my portrait
was somewhat unstable

"No need to fear falling"
the artist waved
"Just keep entirely still
and hold your balance"

I hoisted myself to the platform
becoming so quiet
my drowsy head soon
drooped to my shoulder
then chair, platform and I
clatteringly collapsed

"Oaf, wretch, klutz"
shouted Cézanne
flinging himself at me:
"I told you
to keep still
like an apple

        Does an apple
        fidget?"

After that
when posing
I would swallow
black coffee
fearing the look that signed
        "An apple doesn't move"

How His Colours

breathe azure

        think *noir*

                feel white-of-dusk

flash brushstrokes

        pool

           in the secrets

                  of our abandoned

                        flesh

Hortense

The nineteen-year-old who posed
            for Cézanne in Paris
                        still poses a few questions

Working-class model, bookbinder
            farmer's daughter, main squeeze
                        then mother to Paul Jr.

To his friends, *La Boule*
            dumpling, yet she seems trim
                        enough in his paintings
                                    (affectionate sobriquet or jab?)

to Cézanne's father, his son's clandestine lover
            dubious, long unacknowledged
                        unwelcome at the family estate
                                    then (after 17 years)   spouse
Anecdotes abound:
            she was profligate
                        adored the casinos
                  belittled his art
                        lingered for an appointment with her seamstress
                                    at news of his death
                                                bundled off his paintings for quick sale

Yet what of the hours when
            she sat immobile   silent
                        as he ranged the enigma
                                                of her upper lip
studied her apple faces
            just as he traced the clefts of his holy mountain
                        through dashes and daubs of paint?

What remains of such intimate distances?
            A sleek chignon
                        the sheen of a green-striped skirt
                                    red armchair cupping
the folded hands

Le Père

Blocking figure   foil
                                    pushes his son into law school
                              a kid who excels in literature and Latin

Louis-Auguste   businessman cum banker
                             august indeed in C's portraits

Yet he poses for hours while his son paints
                              subsidizes his bohemian Parisian stays

bestows a share not only of his estate
                              (Jas de Bouffan)
                                            but a grudging respect

So when the artist conjugates the dark
                              around his father's head
he paints *L'Evenement*
                    (a radical newspaper)
                              between the paternal paws
                                            (Cézanne's small joke?)

Years later C remarks:
"My father
          who was a fine man
would say
'You have to play games.'
                    That's what we find in painting"

La Mère

Sombre in black
                              smudged gypsy cheekbones
white kerchief forming a slight widow's peak

Why did he later douse her only portrait
                              in heavy black paint?

Uneducated
          but not illiterate
              she made (Renoir remembered)
                              the best fennel soup
encouraged Paul through nods
                              to press on with his art
his ally against the paternal business shrewdness
                              finding nothing in Paul to disappoint

It's easy to blame him
                    for skipping out of her funeral
yet
on that day   he had to paint
                              just as on every other
trowelling his grief into canvases where morning greys
                              slid into late-afternoon mauves

Some say he was out of sorts
                              with what was expected
dreading most
                    the social encounter

All we know
is that when Hortense burned his mother's effects
                              he stumbled alone on the roadways
                                                for hours

Zola

The childhood inseparables
        swimming   lounging   dreaming
novelist and painter
        raised in Aix

As schoolboys
        Paul protected beleaguered Émile
As adults
        Émile loaned Paul money
           weaving their joint obsessions
           (Flaubert, Baudelaire)
           into his books

Years later   when Zola featured in his novel *L'Oeuvre*
        the figure of a failed, impotent, suicidal
           artist   uncomfortably resembling Cézanne
some wondered if the painter would sulk   flail

Yet when Zola sent him a copy of the *roman*
        C simply penned a polite thanks

(Even before its publication
        they had become a pair of sundered wings)

We may speculate about the breach
        wound /betrayal

yet all we know is
        when told of Zola's death
           Cézanne disappeared into his studio howling

emerged   saying nothing
        diligent only to die painting

      which he finally did

The Son

(based on *Portrait of the Artist's Son*, c. 1880)

I cannot reach the intensity that develops before my senses; I do not possess
that wonderful wealth of colours that enlivens nature ... I believe I could
occupy myself for several months without moving, merely by looking sometimes
more to the right and sometimes more to the left.
      – Cézanne's letter to Paul Jr., Sept. 8 1906

Paul Jr.
      (adored only child
      the artist's "orient")
not a painter
but one in whom the old man confided
      a month before his death

Now in BC
      I find myself listening
morning after morning
      to see what I see
near the snowed-on firs and red cedars
along the banks of the Fraser

where tubular wands of trees
multiply and move
      shift and disappear
into diverse angles
      words can't retrieve

It's for the heroisms of attention
      he'll be remembered

      scent of spruce
            spears of pine

      rising from black rifts in the ground

            to his son's white collar

The Mystery Woman

Who was the mysterious female?
Voiceless   featureless   un-depicted   un-posed   unnamed

Why this mid-life spot-in-time affair
in the life of a man who would later paint himself
into hermit-dom
only wishing to burn each day *sur le motif*?

We know he wrote her one letter:
"I saw you and you let me kiss you"
                              ("seeing," the operative word)

Such electrified torment
the wobbling of marriage vows at forty-six
just another part of the form?

Whether their love was consummated
we'll never know

only that after her assumed rejection
he resumed his longer obsession

to paint alone in *plein air*
                  giving up one perspective
                          for the many

The Housekeeper Madame Brémond: A Complaint

This upstart Canadian *femme* comes to Aix
for only two brief months
all these years later
          thinking she can get closer to the *monsieur* than I
who saw him up at 3 am
so he could trek to the *atelier* to paint

I brined his olives
 picked up his *pâtés*
monitored his diabetes
laid iodine poultices on his chest
tended his swollen right foot

She thinks she knows *le monsieur* better
though I alone was there when he died
          present and accounted for

telegrammed Hortense and Paul Jr.
then   sat and sat
alone   with the flesh
emptied of life
as his precious tubes
                         of cobalt blue
and cadmium yellow

still streaking
          through *Still Life with Milk Jug and Fruit*

                    (the very jug I first hoisted home)

Cézanne's *Sacre Coeur*
(Mont Sainte-Victoire)

With only his walking stick, easel, canvas, paints
   and two good legs, he circled the mountain

painted her eighty-seven times
   wooing her from a thousand angles

His light-sculpted bathers
   softened into a complex attention

Even after summiting (not surmounting)
   he lingered over shadow-greens at her base

   (all the while seeming fierce and monkish to the world) ·

Sometimes her clouds settled so delicately in his mind
   the mauves poured through his hands

At sixty-seven, returning from a *plein air* rendezvous
   he collapsed on the road in a thunderstorm

   (was trundled home in a laundry cart)

Days later   (music of thyme in his limbs)
      they found him asleep in the mountain's arms

Quantum Mountain (*Étude* 1)

The more he tracked, traced
    circled, retraced her traces

the more she seemed to move
    away   almost to disappear

As he gaped   into her sun
    the limestone quarries fractured

her ochre morphed to a glimmering field
    web of trackless vibrating points, violet within of cells

The more she vanished
    the more she seemed to offer entrance

the more elusive her poetry
    the more it was utterly clear

and when he resigned completely
    the gaps opened

linearity, perspective
        failed

leaving only the mountain's mysterious signatures
        places where the witnesses could gather

Lyric Mountain

Tender and apprehensive
      prehensile as the brain's interchanging
            chambers

                so the mountain to Cézanne
      (this late-coming Moses)
            trudging Aixian roads

Not since Sappho, such lyric

      sensualities   arduous scrutiny of time's
                ultraviolet crags

The mountain
      a seascape
            patchwork
                tossed from strophes of light

Even the children
      hurling stones at his barbaric back
             must have felt something meteoric
                streaming from their hands

Quantum Mountain (*Étude* 2)

The more he tracked   circled
retraced her traces   the more she seemed

to move away   almost to
       disappear

When he gaped into her sun
her limestone quarries   /
                          fractured

ochre stone morphed to a glimmering field
uncertain web   vibrating points

quaking interiority of cells

The more she vanished
the more she   seemed
                    to offer entrance

the more elusive her poem
the more it became   utterly clear

So when he resigned   let go completely
of linearity
                           perspective

her gaps
        opened

leaving only the mountain's
               signatures

where (later)
         the witnesses would gather

Poems and Paintings Breathing

Open the spaces   let the mountain begin
       its slow, strange
                            disappearing act
slower than yours
       as the sapphire exceeds the hydrangea   in slow time

Fill her spacecubes with light
Let it drip down mist   onto the canvas

Open the lines   to themselves
        to make room   for the painter's
        crisp, mellow
        pommes
and their absences

Let the image fall into the image-
less
so the painting   the poem
                (these diligences, offerings)
might contain
        more than we know

the swivelling
brown desk chair where a poet
nightscapes small black symbols onto a screen

(or more pointedly)

        the suddenly breathful   olive tree
swaying herself right out of
the artist's visual field

(tree to landscape as landscape
to tree)
extending her arms like a gnarled lover into his colourplanes

        or whatever words
                present

Quantum Mountain (*Étude* 3)

The more he tracks
　　　　　circles
　　　　　　　　　　retraces her traces
the more she seems to move away
　　　　　　　　　　　　　almost
to disappear

When he gapes into her sun
　　　　　　　　her limestone quarries　　/ fracture
ochre stone morphs
　　　　　to a glimmering field

　　　　　vibrating points　　　　　　　uncertain web

　　　　　　　　　　　quaking interiority of cells

The more she vanishes
　　　　　the more she seems to offer entrance
　　　　　　　　　　　　　the more elusive her poem
　　　　the more it becomes　　utterly clear

so when he lets go of linearity
　　　　　　　　perspective
　　　　　her gaps　　　　　open

leave only the mountain's signatures
　　　　　　　　　　where
(later)
　　　　　　　　　　　　　the witnesses gather

So This

is what it is

        to be

a mountain

        (divinity among the pygmies)

to feel their cares

        their small feet gripping down

hands stretching wide

        but not even halfway

(with their eyes)

        around your girth

Who Can Say

who came first to whom?
Yet I think Cézanne and the mountain came to each other
on the selfsame day

on the same wave of longing

(surely they swore an indissoluble oath)

Cézanne lugging down his burning canvas scrolls

Mont Sainte-Victoire and Golden Ears

A stroll each day along the dike by the Fraser River
          where eagles flap, flap, flap   and glide

to their posts in Douglas firs
          near peaks sacred to Coast Salish tribes

Compared to Victoire, the Golden Eyries are enormity
          Snow Queens   dazzling crowns

white beyond froth   beyond bone
          glaciated   cascades

If Cézanne could be airlifted here
          would he be undone?

I see his astounded eyes lower, close
                fling wide

Brush participates in spirals of light
               gaze leans into cliffs' breath

lifts to   falls from
            their icy gowns

He would paint himself into these goddesses
          as they are   who they are

                    who we are in them

Mont Sainte-Victoire and Mount Baker

C keeps painting, this time Baker

adding another range   another seeing
                from this undreamed part of the planet

all the while longing
                for his pine- and oak-ringed Victoire

his Cambrian giant rising when the Pyrenees
                collided with the European plate

Baker   younger   erupted out of earth's core
                a slumbering volcano

Even now, though less majestic
                    Victoire remains his sole *massif*

His *mont* and my mountain
                        precedent   antecedent to

        us   late coming artists and poets

                                        so small yet

so in love

Cézanne's *Baigneuses*

still bathing
            sky falling forever

into their bones
            (chartreuse grasses flowing

around and into
            relaxed limbs)

one leans into a tree
            that leans into her

some touching, others holding themselves   apart
            three here   five over there –

golden numbers
               everywhere   circulating

exactly how the world would look
                  if earth were suddenly

                         to compose our flesh

Finesse

All these strokes accomplished

     by the dark-eyed Provençal

        who sculpted his bathers

   out of

        water   stone   sky

Renouncing the use of nude models

   he found them naked

in himself

In Cézanne's *Les Grandes Baigneuses*

flesh once again sings itself solid
                 where a sapphire river
mates with the hearing eye

Titian   Tintoretto Rubens
                 rise again in oils
from Impressionism's shimmer:
                          sculpted clouds

trees vaulting over flesh's density

the correspondences:
                     taste seeing
                     touch sounding
                          (as Baudelaire sang)

Faces'
             androgynous blurs
                  bodies
                     articulate
                         symmetries
                            in groupings

                                     of five
                                          and eight
rendering poetry and painting
             each other's
                 semblances and *frères*

After seven years' labour
                          he leaves the work

                unfinished

No Still Life Is Still
(on *Jacket on a Chair*, 1892)

The gravity of the garment
                (overcoat, sheath, shroud)
slumps into the gravity of the chair

The garment is full of circles
cylinders and cones

What trembles
in the collar
             is a mountain
                    made of soft charcoal strokes

The heap slides
            floats
in oneness with the chair

grows legs
pretending its human burden
is still there

but the human has flown
though the garment holds
his subtle energies

swirling and overflowing
to become
its own creature
            a new thing

still remembering
human limbs
            the warmth of the painter's back

The garment likes autonomy
Loves to drape itself
            around the unfolding folds
                    of folds

Cézanne's Blues

1907: Rilke haunts the Cézanne retrospective in Paris daily for three weeks

writes his artist wife Clara
                    of his hauntings:
                                "Suddenly one has the right eyes"

not speaking of the ocular nerve
                    but eye of the heart
                                passing among the colours into which the colours are
passing

finding words for spaces where palette and pen converge
                    striving to scribe what Cézanne painted
                                in a parallel dance

Yet how can sideways words hold
                                the visibility
                                of drawn-though-invisible music?

Ut pictura poesis   picture and poem
                                analogues
                                        yet never the same

How can words sound being-in-the-world
                                the way Cézanne's brush touches
                                        bodies and skies?

No grasping can command
                                what presents itself alive
or not at all

so the poet seeks exactness   not description
                    coupled with the indeterminate   the precisely inexact
                                        disappearing act

It was then   hot words poured
                              onto Rilke's white page
              just as Cézanne's blues once washed the canvases
                        the master would sometimes destroy
                              or bury in the earth

              under his beloved mountain

Digging His Blues
(a found poem)

Rilke dug the blues
        in Van Gogh and the Impressionists
                but Cézanne's blues knocked him out

Blues with "good conscience"
            (blues with consciousness)

Blue turnings   tunings   burnings
                    summoned the poet

helped him find the words
        that were always slipping

                          away:

"Egyptian shadow-blue
            self-contained blue
      listening blue
                thunderstorm blue
bourgeois cotton blue
        light cloudy bluishness
            densely quilted blue
waxy blue
      wet dark blue
        juicy blue"

        blue

How the Nazis Lusted After Cézannes

Decades of sneers
           from peers and academy:
then suddenly everyone wants to smuggle
                       loot   snare
a cache or two of Cézannes

Nazis ached for art
           and Hitler   (once-
aspiring artist
           lover of dogs
           and Wagner)
hungered
           for oeuvres
           of the degenerate modernists

One canny Jewish woman
           smuggled hordes of Cézannes to America
                     where they remain prized

War and art always
           such ambivalent pals
since something needs to plunder what allures

Art, that magnetic wave
           to higher thought is
no guarantor of transformation

though sometimes we die
           and are remade
                     by curious swaths of paint
                        smeared on canvas

A Shadowing of Gertrude Stein's Poem "Cézanne"

Every day in Aix is a day daying. Everyone can say every day. In this way I have a place to say that he was met because I did not stay to meet or say. When I said the saying I had meant to stay past Saturday or today. Here two months is a year and a year triples to taste. In this way a mouth opened from oils, pastels, is un-purchasable yet observed. Not observing holidays or holy days but paints full still, still full of water and limbs. The blue waters bled when touched and became precious blue though I remained un-absolved, still believing in water and ghosts. So Cézanne accosted me, crossed my path offering the surprise of honey. He fell in with me on the road so I kept tugging at his coat-tails, which he didn't have, but honey and prayers flowed where the grass blew out of the sidewalks near the Rotunda.

D.H. Lawrence and Apple-ness

Cézanne's Apple rolled the stone from the mouth of the tomb.
      – D.H. Lawrence

Cézanne's work hit Lawrence hard
                              So he took up painting at the age of 40

Some "shiftiness"   in the landscapes
                              held the ever shifting-ness of the world

what L called its "weird anima"
                              the places where things

dematerialize   crystallize   reform

like an apple given back its flesh
                              making baby steps toward matter

                              (which is energy)

"Cézanne's apple hurts"
                  said Lawrence
                        because the artist felt the apple's layers

Despite not being able to find his way
                  back to his own body

                        C let the apple roll away the stone

Cézanne's Doubt

Everything comes to us from nature; we exist through it; nothing else is worth remembering.
   – Paul Cézanne, as cited by Merleau-Ponty

There's something about Cézanne
                that's not charm or grace
something Merleau-Ponty grasped
in his most phenomenological dreams

some need   to taste
the thing painted
                till sight becomes touch

one still life – 100 sessions
one portrait – 150 or more
one brushstroke –
                hours
I too obsess   over poems
forever changing line   breaks   / and spacing

as drafts morph   incessant
under my hooded eyes

Age?
Some congenital perfectionism?

All I know is   I'm in my 67th year
and Cézanne died at 67 (as did my father)

His faithful doubt
                my doubt

that what we love will return
                that the work will be finished

yet   there's always nature
                scintillating   shifting
                            chaos of sensations
just this

Heidegger Comes to the Mountain

These days in Cézanne's home country are worth more than a whole library
of philosophy books. If only one could think as directly as Cézanne painted.
       – Martin Heidegger

What compelled the philosopher to come to Aix
                                                (1956, '57, '58)
numbering its mistrals like time on his pulse?

(Readers layer readers as paints layer paints)

Rilke's letters on Cézanne
                worlded Heidegger
                                (such thinking
                                        turned over like rock
        into ethos)
                        calling up wisdom's deep song

In Aix, the philosopher wrote a poem titled "Cézanne"
                counting the artist a poet
                        then clasped the ghosts of the mountain's
                                        ungraspability

its poem-ing
                        where we
                                hapless thrown ones

can   in turn

        intone
                        and turning
                                                en-poem

                        being

                        (*Dasein*)

Ginsberg's Ports

Black-bearded Ginsberg
        looks a lot like Cézanne
                in C's early self-portraits

Perhaps when the poet wrote "Cézanne's Ports"
he heard the artist speaking
just as the Beat poet heard William Blake
                in a vision of his youth

Everyone   (it seems)
                        wanted to be Cézanne
or to be inside Cézanne
or to be Cézanne's process –

that blue fuse

In "The Gulf of Marseilles seen from L'Estaque"
Allen notes:

            the artist's red tile roofs
                    flip like a deck of cards
                            under a terrific sun

Suzanne de Cézanne Overhears a Monologue from Heaven by Thomas Merton de Cézanne

My father painted like Cézanne and understood the southern French landscape the way Cézanne did.
– Thomas Merton, The Seven-Storey Mountain

I was born in Prades
under the Pyrenees
in the year of the Waterbearer

My parents were bohemian artists
who met in art school
travelled around the countryside
painting   before the war intervened

When I wrote *My Argument with the Gestapo*
a print of Cézanne's Mont Sainte-Victoire
hung over the bed of my protagonist
like a great cloud of unknowing

At my uncle's in England
I didn't have to hide
my view that the Modernists
                 weren't nuts

Social Realism left me cold
         but I got impressions

In '39
I riffed to friend Bob Lax:

okay more tinsel
thoughts from the Museum
of Modern Art
Oh boy some Picasso
called seated woman oh boy

some picasso hoyhoy
dancedance
hoyhoyhoy
similar dances
for the cézannes
                    good yeah, fine

I'm quoted saying Picasso was the greatest
but qualified
                    "with the exception of Cézanne"

I seconded Paul Tillich:
"There's more of ultimate reality
in an apple by Cézanne
than in a Jesus by Hoffman"

and would have written
an *oeuvre*
on the Modernist painters
                    but just didn't have the time

In the end
                    it's about beauty

the way his mountain
falls through sky
and clods of earth
fall through
the mountain

the way his studies
hold
          sky and ground
his time and mine
                    in a mountain's hush

Renewing Language

Cézanne had to forge a new language, abandoning linear and aerial perspective
and making the spatial dispositions arise from the modulations of colour.
    – Charles Taylor, *Sources of the Self*

His paintings are an afterlife
        of inter-dimensional planes

if we allow them
in   (the in of out   out of in)

Therefore
      we are not done with him

or he with us
since a new language

is a new species

      Trickster yellow
          Palaeolithic red

chimed with the stomp of dinosaurs
      who wandered

Mont Sainte-Victoire's slopes
         leaving fossilized eggs

He taught us we are egg men
      egg women   *mandorlas*

letting the world take us in
        from so many mysterious
             angles

Cézanne's Geological Practice

[T]he geological foundations slowly reveal themselves to me, the layers establish
themselves, the great planes of my canvas, in my mind I draw the stony skeleton.
  – Paul Cézanne (from a letter to Joachim Gasquet)

At the Bibémus Quarries
where Cézanne came to sketch
        I tilted
            among boulders

peered through red-orange
skystreams
whose violets and blues
loped into matter

and stayed
for a while
then gravitied to
anti-matter

dark holes
where there is
no still life
where no life is still

The dazzling chaos
he served
held my eyes
in a geometrical trance

no flesh
but the flesh of melting
stone

and the wind
huff puffing

ochre rising from the abyss
        between
              vast transparent   windows

Cézanne's Ecological Practice

The two artists painted together in the open air
                                        under the mountain
                                        side by side

Renoir's paintings
are warmer   much prettier than Cézanne's

(which is not to disparage R's
                    impressions of lovely woman
his diffuse reflections on
                    glowing-cheek pinks
and streaming-hair reds)

Yet Renoir
bowed to Cézanne's ecological practice

noting how C would sometimes return his art to the earth

                                        as offerings

Cézanne Camouflaged
(based on a black and white photo of the artist)

The figure gazes out-
side &   in-side

                              out
                resting among

Aleppo pines
ferns
              quarried stone

                    a solitude man
in black and white

held
in a camera's clasp

absorbed by filtering sun

black coat
black felt bowler
                    hunkered
on the ground

where he casts
a spare eye

sideways
over the rim

                    of spring's slope

a firmness   barely seen
but pressing in

                    to morning
weather

Around
his squat frame:

                    the all-surpassing

                                   wild

On Attending the Hungarian Sinfonetta's *Stabat Mater* Concert
(Église Saint Espirit, Aix-en-Provence)

Sitting in the nave with Cézanne
      who here   regularly   unaccountably attended mass
          (convention?   some deeper call?)

I wonder who wouldn't turn to music –
                       this tingling in the cells

this tiptoeing to the beginning
               of waterfalls

               footfalls

where musical time is
               hypnogogic

where wonder wanders
               extending her grace notes?

What calls us to compress
               the joy that makes us

               fearless

in the integral scale's tensions
                    and rests

        unbroken broken

               measures

               falling through paints

                  and words

Leaning Together

Violin trails lift me to my husband

                    in British Columbia

his night   my morning

              our absence from one another:

          grist of transformation

Harpsichord strews gold notes

             on his pillow

as I hear what together

               (and distanced)

          makes a music

On Hearing an Organ Concert of Bach's Brandenburg Concerto No. 5 in D Major
(Église Saint Jean de Malte, Aix-en-Provence)

Poet and painter perch   side by side

                     swept into the cadences

No apparent scheme

                  yet a *motif* returns

like stars

          scintillating

A beat   clearly not the metronome's

               but heart's drum

fugue's complicated

          counterpointings

in the small of the ear

                heaven's simple doorway

where words and colours

             toss

My Father's Final Words

Cézanne and my father:
>   such gentleness
>   from such brooders

After all these years Dad's last words
>   clean on air:

Enjoy your life:
>   *these passing cares will pass –*

press inward to the joy

Beware: Serious Tree Hugger

*The olive tree was waiting for him ... He would touch it. He would talk to it.
When he parted from it at night he would sometimes embrace it ... The wisdom
of the tree entered his heart. "It's a living being," he said to me one day. "I love it
like an old friend. It knows everything about my life and gives me excellent advice.
I should like to be buried at its feet."*
     – Henri Gasquet

They all painted olive trees
                     Matisse, Monet
Van Gogh   a whole grove of them outside Arles
twisting now as it did when Vincent first came
to the sanatorium

But of Cézanne alone was it said
he spoke to his olive
touched and embraced her
savouring her salt
in thick *beures blanches*
over chicken or duck

I thought of him at the *marchés* in Aix
when I brought home bagfuls
of the small, black ones

like those perhaps from the olive
at his studio at Les Lavres

for he bought the land
precisely because of the tree

Despite C's request
he was not buried under the olive
but buries and raises himself daily
                 in his olive tree paintings

"He had no real friends except trees"
          said his friend Henri

Embracing Trees

Home in Fort Langley
I race to the big Douglas Fir
gracing my kitchen window
roots gripping into the ravine

host to step moss, lichen
and pileated woodpeckers

recalling how once I named
this unnameable, un-own-able one
"Victorine"   the victorious
long before I laid eyes
        on Cézanne's olives
                        under Sainte-Victoire

In a Mind Clench with Cézanne

Night after night   lines   from unwritten
                poems he inspires
                              wake me

One (insistent)
                sprawls across the bed
                          till I resign

to this mind-heart-soul-clench   with Paul Cézanne

I lug myself up
                stumble to the kitchen
                  grapple for a pen
                    put on the light
                      scrawl words

The incipient poem
            a wholeness
                that doesn't require me
                      (so why am I here?)
The gift
        broken phrases
                with nothingness
                      in between
leaving

the almost impossible task
        of finding connections
          like sturdy Roman bridges
              arched across Provence

One poem suggesting a wholeness
        to another   who will also enter
                     compresence

(I want to make one poem
            as real as his apples)

The Power of Vegetables

"With an apple
I will
astonish
Paris"
said Paul Cézanne

though it wasn't just the apple
but the many seeings
one perspective from the right
another from the left

another from above
another from below
and so on
all in one apple

cross-dimensionality of appleness
in an ordinary apple
one might use for pies
or apple sauce

"The day is
coming
when a single
carrot

freshly observed
will set off
a revolution"
he quipped

I'm still revolving in my dreams
   the matter of the carrot

The Gardener Vallier Speaks

Under the lime tree in the garden
he painted me again

a few days after they brought him home
when he fell on the road in a storm

So many hours I had posed for him
not minding the passage of time

the long breaks from work
occasions to sit quietly remembering this and that

We talked some
but mostly we worked in silence

and I remember
how I bought him herbs

massaged his limbs
when he wouldn't let anyone else touch him

I, the only one there when he died

Some say he painted himself
into me and I entered him

our beards and peasant hats
the dark background against a white shirt

crossed legs
                the gentle flow of hands

On Cézanne's *Study of a Skull*

A troop of skulls
            still lines   a wall
                                in his Les Lauves studio
haunt for our "Alas, poor Yorick" moments

At twenty   my own brevity
                        flipped rarely through my head
but now with parents aunts uncles friends gone
                    memento mori settles in

here where the charcoal smudge
                      in Cézanne's sketch
                      backdrops the white dome of bone
                      that once housed a head

where consciousness
         seems to hover –
though these days
             dances more often in my toes, feet, belly
                along the ridge of the spine

His drawing
             floats on a host of mountains
                  the skull a passing thing
among things passing
             one eye   a shaded door

The creature I am
            seems to feel what it will be like
                to release   my weary personality
with its shallow coves

Cézanne's skull kindly lends me
                its full regard
wistfully querying:
         "Who will you be

when what you think you see
         in the mirror flies away
              and memory pours out
                     its casket of jewels?"

The Power of the Vow
(a found poem by Cézanne)

I always study
>
> from nature

and it seems to me

> I am making slow progress but

I am old and

> ill

I have vowed

to die painting

rather than to sink

into the degrading

> senility

> [that]

> threatens the old people

> who let themselves

be ruled by passions

[that]

> dull

> the senses

Such a Proceeding

Out of emergency

      the poems & paintings emerge

         simply there

              whistling

    from songbird's beak

      blue

            transparent

                      gone

Acknowledgements

I can do no better than to cite Cézanne's biographer Alex Danchev: "We shall never have done with Cézanne. I can think of no higher praise."

My gratitude extends to the following who assisted in the birth, nurturance, and production of this cycle:

Allan Briesmaster, publisher and editor of Quattro Books, for believing in this sequence, and for his thoughtful and meticulous editing of the text

To everyone on the Quattro team, and to copy editor Sarah Varnam, for seeing this manuscript through its various stages

E.D. Blodgett, who helped me discover the silences in the words, the words in the silences, and above all, to wait for the music

David Zieroth, who first published a subset of these poems for his Alfred Gustav Poetry Series (North Vancouver, British Columbia, 2015)

J.S. Porter, poet, essayist, and friend from Hamilton, Ontario, who was the first person (besides myself) to lay eyes on any of these poems

Antoinette Voûte Roeder, soul friend and fellow poet, whose early comments and encouragement set me in the right direction

Katerina Fretwell and Penn Kemp, friends and fellow poets who put up with my barrage of emailed Cézanne poems when they had to deal with more pressing concerns

My women's writing group Memoir-sistas, fellow servants of the Muse of language and longing: Kate Braid, Heidi Greco, Joy Kogawa, Elsie Neufeld, and Marlene Schiwy

To my poetry reading group, The Compossibles

To my long-time friend, dancer, educator and poet, Celeste Snowber

To my friend Erica Grimm, visual artist extraordinaire

To fellow poet Leslie Timmins, who inspired me with her work on Matisse and helped with some fine-tuning of the early poems from this sequence

To Jennifer Zilm, my former student at Douglas College, whose poems on Van Gogh in her chapbook *the whole and broken yellows* confirmed the value of revisiting the Modernist painters

And to my family, my husband Mark Haddock and daughter Claire Haddock for their ongoing support and encouragement

The following poems have been published or accepted for publication:

"On Coming Late to the Shock of Modernism," in *The Crooked Ledge of Another Day: An Anthology of Bizarre Prose and Poetry*. Ed. David Fraser. Nanaimo, B.C.: Ascent Aspirations Publishing, 2014, 53.

"The Progress of His Turbulence," "Zola," "So This," "Who Can Say?" and "The Task," in *HA&L (Hamilton Arts and Letters) Magazine*, Issue 7:2, Dec. 2014 Online. http://samizdatpress.typepad.cohal magazine-issue-seven-2/poetry-by-susan-mccaslin-2.html

"Mont Sainte-Victoire and Mount Baker" and "Cézanne's Lyric Mountain," in *Cascadia Review* with "Statement of Place," Jan.-Feb. 2015. Online. http://cascadiareview.org/category/susan-mccaslin/

"Cézanne's Apples," "I Close My Eyes," "*Le Père*," "Hortense," "*LaMère*," "The Housekeeper Madame Bermond: a Complaint," "The Gardener Vallier Speaks," "Cézanne's *Baigneuses*," "Quantum Mountain (*Étude* 1)," "Cézanne's Sacre Coeur," and "Cézanne's Doubt," in the chapbook, *effortful / effortless: after Cézanne*, ed. David Zieroth. North Vancouver, BC: The Alfred Gustav Press, May 2015.

"The Power of Vegetables," "Seeing Seeing," & "Epistolary Poetics," in *Make It True: Poems from Cascadia*. Ed. Paul Nelson. Lanzville, B.C.: Leaf Press, 2015.

"In Cézanne's *Les Grandes Baigneuses*," in *The Ekphrastic Review: writing and art on art and writing*. Publisher/editor Lorette C. Luzajic. 21 April, 2016. Online. www.ekphrastic.net

"Heidegger Comes to the Mountain," in *Canadian Literature: A Quarterly of Criticism and Review*, Number 255 (Summer 2015), 10. Also published online: https://canlit.ca/wp-content/uploads/2016/05/McCaslin_225.pdf

Notes

"Exacting Exactitude," p. 23. This incident is based on an account in Tristan L. Klingson's biography *Cézanne* (London: John Lane, the Bodley Head, 1923) 46-47.

"D.H. Lawrence and Apple-ness," p. 51. D.H. Lawrence's citations are drawn from *Poets on Painters: Essays on the Art of Painting by Twentieth-century Poets*, ed. J.D. McClatchy (Los Angeles: University of California Press, 1988).

"Beware: Serious Tree Hugger," p. 65. Alex Danchev, *Cézanne: a Life* (New York: Pantheon Books, 2012) 330.

"The Power of the Vow," p. 71. Cézanne in a letter to his friend Émile Bernard, quoted in Danchev, 333.

Other Recent Quattro Poetry Books